# MASSES AND MOTETS

*Giovanni Pierluigi da Palestrina*

Based on Raffaele Casimiri's Edition

DOVER PUBLICATIONS, INC.

NEW YORK

This Dover edition, first published in 1993,
is a republication of works from the Kalmus reprint (n.d.)
of Volumes III, IV, V, VI, VII, X, XXV and XXIX of
*Le opere complete di Giovanni Pierluigi da Palestrina,*
edited by Raffaele Casimiri,
published by Fratelli Scalera, 1939–1965, in 32 volumes.
A new table of contents and Publisher's Note have been added.
The publisher is grateful to Saul Novack for selecting the works to be included,
and to W. W. Norton & Company, Inc.,
for permission to reprint the tune and words of "L'Homme Armé,"
from Donald J. Grout: *A History of Western Music (Revised Edition),*
copyright © 1973, 1960 by W. W. Norton & Company, Inc.

Manufactured in the United States of America
Dover Publications, Inc.
31 East Second Street
Mineola, NY 11501

*Library of Congress Cataloging-in-Publication Data*

Palestrina, Giovanni Pierluigi da, ca. 1525–1594.
[Vocal music. Selections]
Masses and motets : based on Raffaele Casimiri's edition /
Giovanni Pierluigi da Palestrina.
1 score.
Selections from the Kalmus reprint of: Le opere complete di
Giovanni Pierluigi da Palestrina / edited by R. Casimiri (originally
published by Fratelli Scalera, 1939–1965).
Contents: Missa Ave Regina coelorum : Mass for 4 voices — Veni
sponsa Christi : motet for 4 voices — Missa Veni sponsa Christi :
Mass for 4 voices — O magnum mysterium : motet for 6 voices —
Ascendo ad Patrem : motet for 5 voices — Missa Ascendo ad Patrem :
Mass for 5 voices — Missa L'homme armé : Mass for 5 voices — Missa
Papae Marcelli : Mass for 6 voices.

ISBN 0-486-27631-7

1. Masses, Unaccompanied—Scores.   2. Motets.   I. Casimiri,
Raffaele, 1880–1943.   II. Palestrina, Giovanni Pierluigi da, ca.
1525–1594. Masses. Selections. 1993.   III. Palestrina, Giovanni
Pierluigi da, ca. 1525–1594. Motets. Selections. 1993.
M3.1.P25V6   1993                               93-17230
                                                CIP
                                                M

# CONTENTS

# PUBLISHER'S NOTE

The music of Giovanni Pierluigi da Palestrina (1525–1594) not only represents the culmination of the composition of polyphonic settings of the Roman Mass, but may have even been responsible for safeguarding the place of polyphony in the Church. There is a legend that the Council of Trent (1545–63), in an attempt to "purify" the music of the Church, very nearly abolished polyphony altogether until Palestrina composed a six-voice mass to show that polyphony did indeed have a place in the liturgy and was not at odds with the reverence due the solemn celebration of the Mass. On hearing this mass the Council concurred, thus making Palestrina the "savior" of church music. The mass in question was the "Pope Marcellus" mass (*Papae Marcelli*), contained in the present collection. As a result, Palestrina's music has been held up as a model of composition for the Church right up to our own time.

Coming at the end of 200 years of polyphonic mass composition, Palestrina was indeed master of all the styles in favor among composers. The masses contained herein represent almost all of these styles.

Quite common was the Paraphrase Mass, which relied on a piece of Gregorian Chant for its thematic material. The *Missa Ave Regina Coelorum* (p. 1) is derived from the final anthem of the Office of Compline for the period February 2 until Wednesday of Holy Week:

TRANSLATION: *All hail, Queen of heaven; all hail, Mistress of the Angels. Hail, root; hail, door, from whom a light has risen for the world. Rejoice, glorious Virgin, lovely beyond all others. Farewell, O most beautiful, and plead for us to Christ.*

The following three masses in this collection, *Veni Sponsa Christi* (p. 33), *O Magnum Mysterium* (p. 66) and *Ascendo ad Patrem* (p. 114), are all of the type known as Parody Mass. In this form of composition, another polyphonic work is used as the germ material from which the mass is composed. In the case of these masses, the base works are all motets of Palestrina's own composition. These motets are here included immediately preceding the mass to which their name is given. Of special interest are both "O Magnum Mysterium" and "Ascendo ad Patrem," where material from the Prima Pars of the motet is used for some movements, while the Secunda Pars serves as the basis for the remainder of the mass setting.

The *Missa L'Homme Armé* (p. 148) is one of a long line of masses composed on this famous melody, beginning with Guillaume Dufay or even earlier. This style of composition is known as Cantus Firmus or Tenor Mass ("Tenor" being the word used to denote "Melody" in early Western music). In Palestrina's period of composition, such a melody could be used in any voice, or even in multiple voices to provide thematic unity. This ancient folk melody is provided below:

TRANSLATION: *The armed man is to be feared. Everywhere it has been proclaimed that everyone should arm himself with an iron coat of mail.*

The final composition style represented in the present volume is the so-called Free-Composed Mass. In this type of work, no preexisting melodic or polyphonic material is used, the motifs being originally composed for the mass setting. The *Missa Papae Marcelli* (p. 187), arguably Palestrina's most famous, is just such a setting, having no known basis in previous material. The freedom of invention accorded to the composer is evident in this, one of the most sublime of all polyphonic settings of the Mass.

It will be noted that some text in the masses is given in brackets or italics. These methods were used by the editor to denote text not found in the original sources, but implied by rules of repetition common in Palestrina's day. The accidentals shown in parentheses are editorial reconstructions of the common practice of ficta.

## A Note on Performance

As was the practice of his time, Palestrina did not set the opening phrases of the "Gloria" or "Credo." These incipits were to be intoned by a priest or cantor, the choir continuing with the second phrase. There were many Gregorian melodies available for these incipits, most of which may be found in the *Liber Usualis*. The most common forms are provided below:

In liturgical usage, it is expected that Agnus Dei I will be repeated to allow for the full declamation of the text "Agnus Dei."

# TEXTS AND TRANSLATIONS

## The Masses

### Kyrie

Kyrie eleison.
Christe eleison.
Kyrie eleison.

### Gloria

(Gloria in excelsis Deo,)
et in terra pax hominibus bonae voluntatis.
　　Laudamus te. Benedicimus te.
Adoramus te.
Glorificamus te.
Gratias agimus tibi propter magnam gloriam tuam.
Domine Deus, Rex coelestis, Deus Pater omnipotens.
　　Domine Fili unigenite, Jesu Christe.
Domine Deus, Agnus Dei, Filius Patris.
Qui tollis peccata mundi, miserere nobis.

Qui tollis peccata mundi, suscipe deprecationem nostram.

Qui sedes ad dexteram Patris, miserere nobis.

　　Quoniam tu solus sanctus.
Tu solus Dominus.
Tu solus altissimus, Jesu Christe.
Cum Sancto Spiritu, in gloria Dei Patris.
Amen.

### Credo

(Credo in unum Deum,)
Patrem omnipotentem,
factorem coeli et terrae,
visibilium omnium, et invisibilium.
　　Et in unum Dominum Jesum Christum,
Filium Dei unigenitum.

### Kyrie

Lord, have mercy on us.
Christ, have mercy on us.
Lord, have mercy on us.

### Gloria

(Glory to God in the highest,)
and on earth peace to men of good will.
　　We praise thee. We bless thee.
We adore thee.
We glorify thee.
We give thanks to thee for thy great glory.
Lord God, heavenly King, God the Father almighty.
　　Lord, the only-begotten Son, Jesus Christ.
Lord God, Lamb of God, Son of the Father.
Thou that takest away the sins of the world, have mercy upon us.
Thou that takest away the sins of the world, receive our prayer.
Thou that sittest at the right hand of the Father, have mercy upon us.
　　For thou only art holy.
Thou only art the Lord.
Thou only art most high, Jesus Christ.
With the Holy Spirit, in the glory of God the Father.
Amen.

### Creed (Nicene)

(I believe in one God,)
the Father almighty,
maker of heaven and earth,
of all things visible and invisible.
　　And in one Lord, Jesus Christ,
the only-begotten Son of God.

Et ex Patre natum ante omnia saecula.

Deum de Deo, lumen de lumine,

Deum verum de Deo vero.

Genitum, non factum,

consubstantialem Patri:

per quem omnia facta sunt.

Qui propter nos homines, et propter nostram salutem

descendit de coelis.

Et incarnatus est de Spiritu Sancto,

ex Maria Virgine:

et homo factus est.

Crucifixus etiam pro nobis, sub Pontio Pilato,

passus, et sepultus est.

Et resurrexit tertia die secundum Scripturas.

Et ascendit in coelum,

sedet ad dexteram Patris.

Et iterum venturus est cum gloria judicare vivos et mortuos:

cujus regni non erit finis.

    Et in Spiritum Sanctum, Dominum, et vivificantem:

qui ex Patre Filioque procedit.

Qui cum Patre et Filio simul adoratur, et conglorificatur:

qui locutus est per Prophetas.

Et unam sanctam catholicam et apostolicam Ecclesiam.

Confiteor unum baptisma in remissionem peccatorum.

Et exspecto resurrectionem mortuorum.

Et vitam venturi saeculi.

Amen.

And was born of the Father before all ages.

God of God, light of light,

true God from true God.

Begotten, not made,

Of one Being with the Father:

by whom all things were made.

Who for us men and for our salvation

came down from heaven.

And was made incarnate by the Holy Spirit,

of the Virgin Mary:

and was made man.

He was crucified for us under Pontius Pilate,

suffered, and was buried.

And rose again on the third day, according to the Scriptures.

And ascended into heaven,

and is seated at the right hand of the Father.

And he will come again in glory to judge the living and the dead:

and his kingdom will have no end.

    And [I believe] in the Holy Spirit, the Lord, the giver of life:

who proceedeth from the Father and the Son.

Who with the Father and the Son together is worshiped and glorified:

who hath spoken by the Prophets.

And [I believe in] one holy catholic and apostolic Church.

I confess one baptism for the remission of sins.

And I await the resurrection of the dead.

And the life of the world to come.

Amen.

## Sanctus

Sanctus, sanctus, sanctus, Domine Deus Sabaoth,
Pleni sunt coeli et terra gloria tua.
Hosanna in excelsis.

## Sanctus

Holy, holy, holy, Lord God of Hosts.
Heaven and earth are full of thy glory.
Hosanna in the highest.

## Benedictus

Benedictus qui venit in nomine Domini.
Hosanna in excelsis.

## Benedictus

Blessed is he that cometh in the name of the Lord.
Hosanna in the highest.

## Agnus Dei I

Agnus Dei, qui tollis peccata mundi:
miserere nobis.

## Agnus Dei I

Lamb of God, who takest away the sins of the world:
have mercy upon us.

## Agnus Dei II

Agnus Dei, qui tollis peccata mundi:
dona nobis pacem.

## Agnus Dei II

Lamb of God, who takest away the sins of the world:
grant us peace.

# Veni Sponsa Christi

Veni sponsa Christi, accipe coronam, quam tibi
Dominus praeparavit in aeternum.

Come, you who are betrothed to Christ, accept the
crown which the Lord has prepared for you since
before time.

# O Magnum Mysterium

### Prima Pars

O magnum mysterium, et admirabile sacramentum,
ut animalia viderent Dominum natum, jacentem in
praesepio. Natum vidimus, et choros Angelorum
collaudantes Dominum. Alleluja.

### First Part

O great mystery and wonderful sacrament, in that
the animals have seen the Lord born, and laid in a
manger. We have seen his birth, and choirs of
Angels praising the Lord together. Alleluia.

### Secunda Pars

Quem vidistis, pastores? dicite: annuntiate nobis,
quis apparuit? Natum vidimus, et choros Angelorum
collaudantes Dominum. Alleluja.

### Second Part

Whom have you seen, shepherds? speak and tell us:
who has appeared? We have seen his birth, and
choirs of Angels praising the Lord together. Alleluia.

# Ascendo ad Patrem

### Prima Pars

Ascendo ad patrem meum, et patrem vestrum:
alleluja. Deum meum, et Deum vestrum, alleluja: et
dum assumptus fuero a vobis, mittam vobis Spiritum
veritatis, et gaudebit cor vestrum. Alleluja.

### First Part

I will ascend to my father, and your father: alleluia.
[To] my God, and your God, alleluia: and when I
have been taken away from you, I will send you the
Spirit of truth, and your hearts shall rejoice. Alleluia.

### Secunda Pars

Ego rogabo Patrem, et alium Paracletum dabit vobis
Spiritum veritatis, et gaudebit cor vestrum. Alleluja.

### Second Part

I will ask the Father, and he will give you another
Counselor—the Spirit of truth, and your hearts
shall rejoice. Alleluia.

# MASSES AND MOTETS

# Missa Ave Regina Coelorum

## *MASS FOR 4 VOICES*

### Kyrie

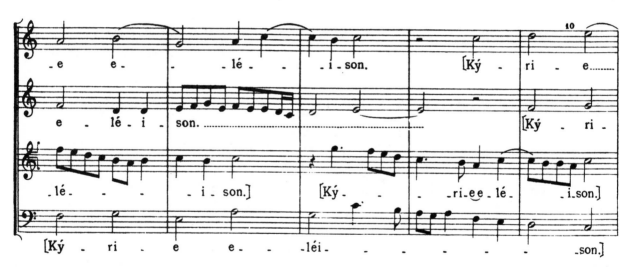

# Gloria

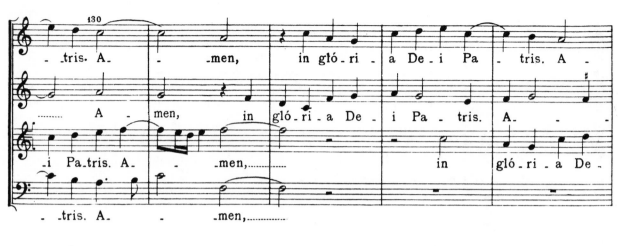

## Credo

# Sanctus

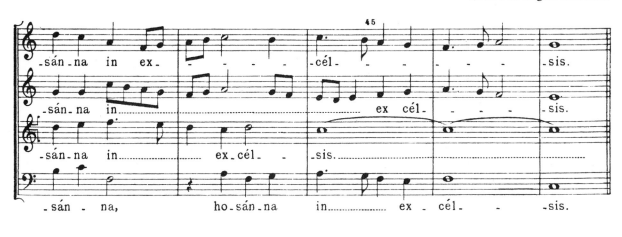

-sán_na in ex_ _ _ _cél_ _ _ _ _sis.

-sán_na in _ _ _ _ _ _ _ ex cél_ _ _ _sis.

-sán_na in_ _ _ _ _ _ ex_cél_ _sis.

-sán_na, ho_sán_na in_ _ _ _ _ _ ex _ cél _ _ _sis.

# Benedictus

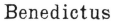

Cum Tribus vocibus

**CANTUS**

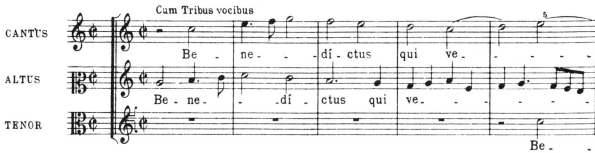

Be _ ne _ _ dí_ctus qui ve _ _ _ _

**ALTUS**

Be _ ne _ _ dí _ ctus qui ve_ _ _ _ _ _

**TENOR**

Be _ _

_ _nit, be_ne_dí _ ctus qui ve _ _nit_ _ _ _ _ _

_ _ _ _nit, be _ ne _ _dí_ctus qui ve_ _ _ _ _

_ne_ _ _dí_ctus qui ve_ _ _ _ _ _ _

in nó_mi _ ne_ _ _ _ Dó_ _ _ _ _ _ _mi _ ni, in nó_mi _

_nit in nó_mi_ne_ _ _ _ Dó _ _ _ _ _ _mi _ ni,

_ _ _ _ _ _nit in nó_mi _ ne_ _ _

_ne_ _ _ _ Dó _ _ _ _mi _ ni, in nó_mi _ ne,_ _ _

in nó _ mine,_ _ _ _ in nó_mi _ ne_ _ Do_

Do_ _ _ _ _ _ _ _mi _ ni, in nó_mi _ ne_ _ _ Dó_ _

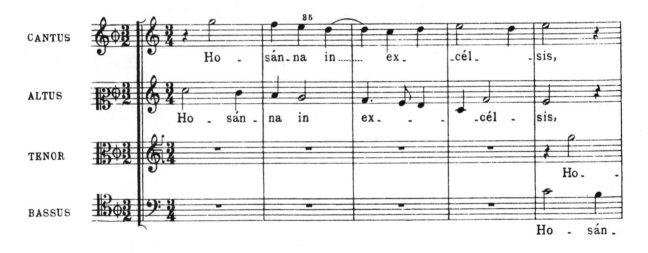

CANTUS

ALTUS

TENOR

BASSUS

## Agnus Dei I

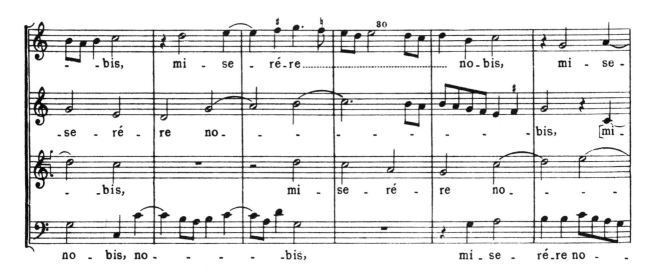

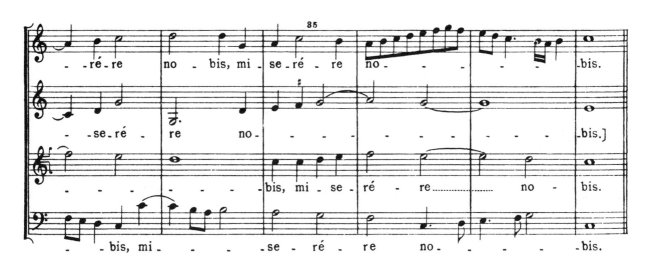

## Agnus Dei II

# Veni Sponsa Christi

## *MOTET FOR 4 VOICES*

# Missa Veni Sponsa Christi

## *MASS FOR 4 VOICES*

### Kyrie

# Gloria

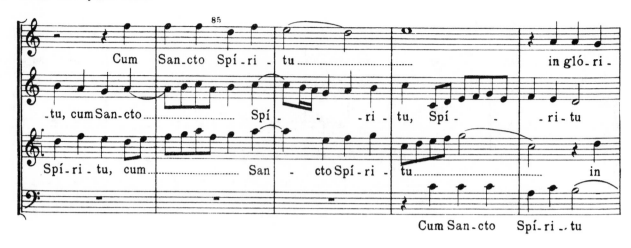

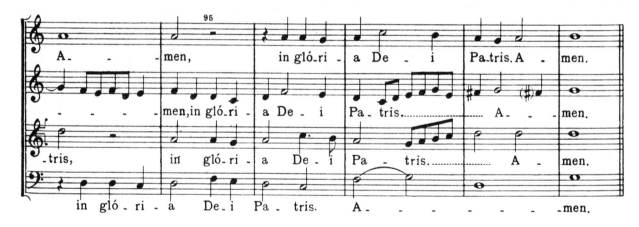

## Credo

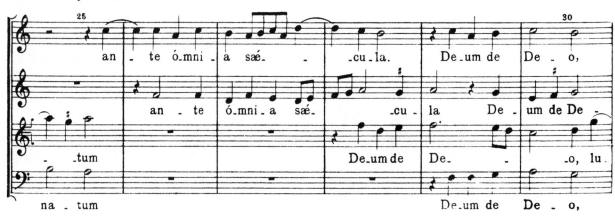

an _ te ó_mni _ a saé _ _cu_la. De_um de De _ o,

an _ te ó_mni_a saé _ _cu_la De _ um de De _

_tum       De_um de De _ _o, lu_

na _ tum               De_um de De _ o,

lu _ men de lú_mi_ne, De _ um ve _ rum de De_o ve _ ro.

_o,       lu_men de lú_mi_ne. De_um ve_rum de De_o ve _ ro.

_men de lú _ mi _ ne, De _ um ve _ rum de De_o ve_ro.

lu_men de lú_mi _ ne,   De _ um   ve _ rum de De_o ve _ ro. Gé _ ni_

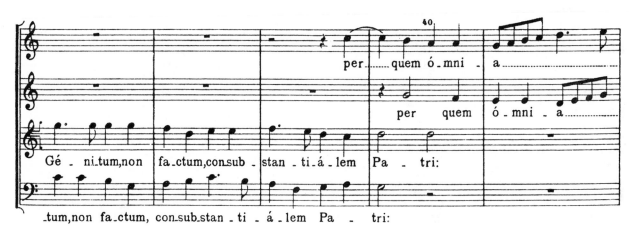

per _____ quem ó_mni _ a _____

per quem ó_mni _ a _____

Gé _ ni_tum,non fa_ctum,con_sub_stan _ ti_á_lem Pa _ tri:

_tum,non fa_ctum, con_sub_stan _ ti _ á _ lem Pa _ tri:

_____ fa _ cta sunt.Qui pro_pter nos hó_mi _ nes,   et pro_pter no _

_____ fa _ cta sunt.Qui pro_pter nos hó_mi _ nes,   et pro_pter no_stram

Qui pro_pter nos hó_mi _ nes, et pro_pter no_

Qui   pro_pter nos hó_mi _ nes,   et pro_pter no _

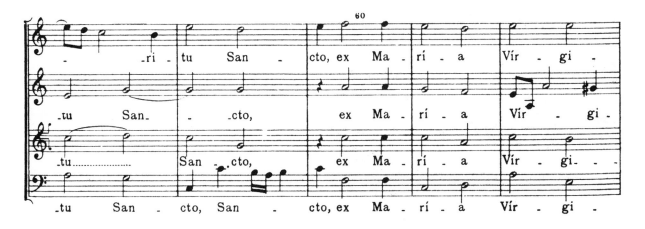

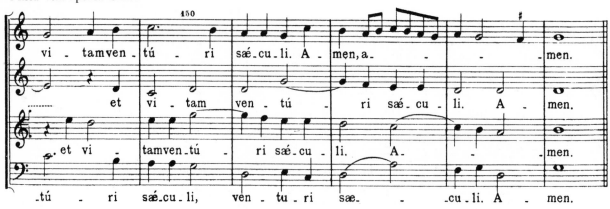

vi _ tam ven _ tú _ ri  saé _ cu _ li. A _ men, a _ _ _ _ men.

et  vi _ tam  ven _ tú _ ri  saé _ cu _ li.  A _ men.

_ et  vi _ tam ven _ tú _ ri saé _ cu _ li.  A _ _ men.

_ tú _ ri  saé _ cu _ li,  ven _ tu _ ri  sae _ _ _ cu _ li. A _ men.

## Sanctus

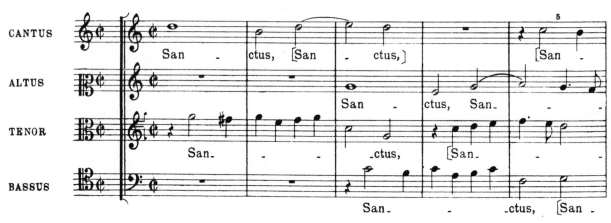

CANTUS  San _ ctus, [San _ ctus,]  [San _

ALTUS  San _ ctus, San _ _

TENOR  San _ _ _ ctus, [San _ _

BASSUS  San _ _ ctus, [San _

_ _ ctus,] _ _ _ _ _ [San _ _

_ _ _ ctus,  [San _ _

_ ctus,]  [San _ _ _ _ ctus,]  [San

_ _ ctus,]  [San _ _ ctus,]

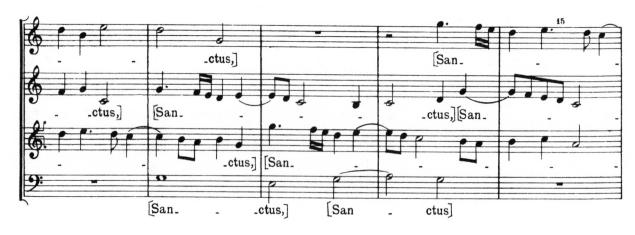

_ _ ctus,]  [San _ _ ctus, San _

_ ctus,]  [San _ _ ctus,][San _

_ ctus,] [San _ _ _

[San _ _ ctus,]  [San _ ctus]

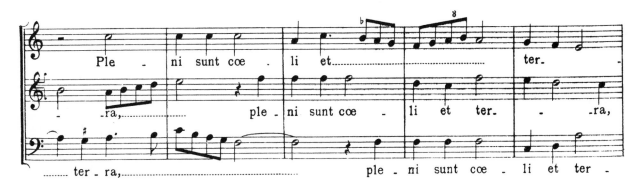

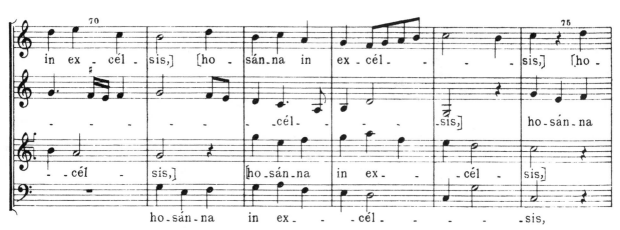

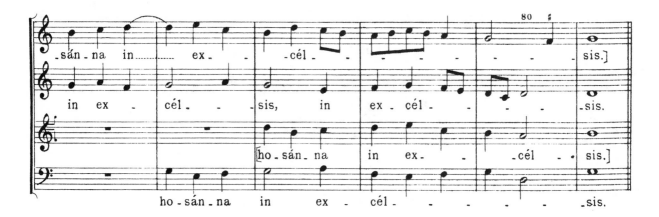

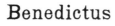

## Benedictus

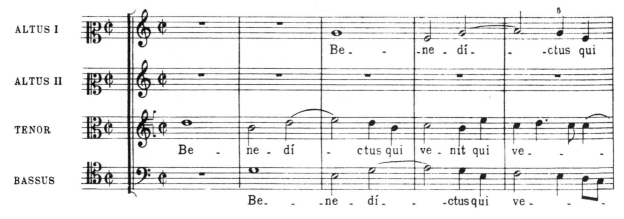

## Agnus Dei I

# Agnus Dei II

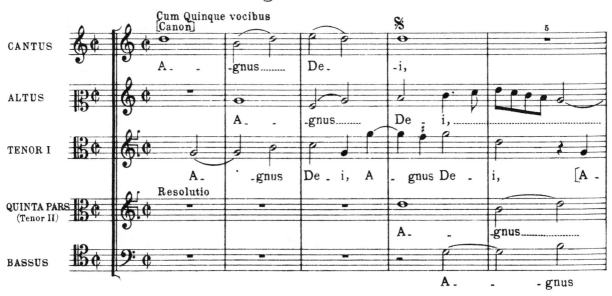

# O Magnum Mysterium

*MOTET FOR 6 VOICES*

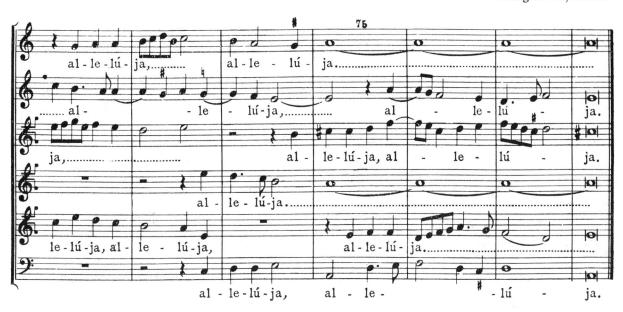

# Missa O Magnum Mysterium

*MASS FOR 5 VOICES*

### Kyrie.

## Kyrie alter. [1]

[1] Ex Cod. 57 Archivii Capellæ Sixtinæ.

## Gloria.

## Credo.

# Sanctus.

# Benedictus.

## Hosanna II.[1]

(1) Ex Cod. 57 Archivii Capellæ Sixtinæ.

# Agnus Dei I.

## Agnus Dei II.

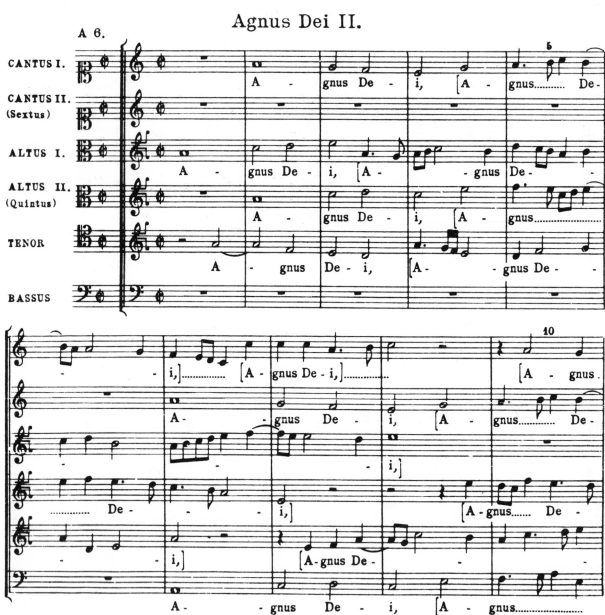

# Ascendo ad Patrem

## *MOTET FOR 5 VOICES*

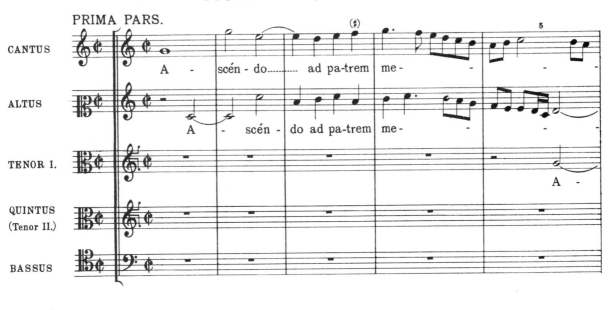

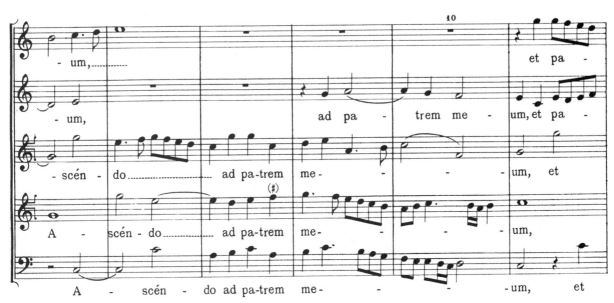

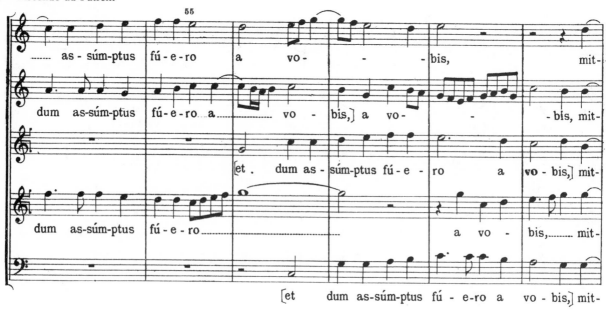

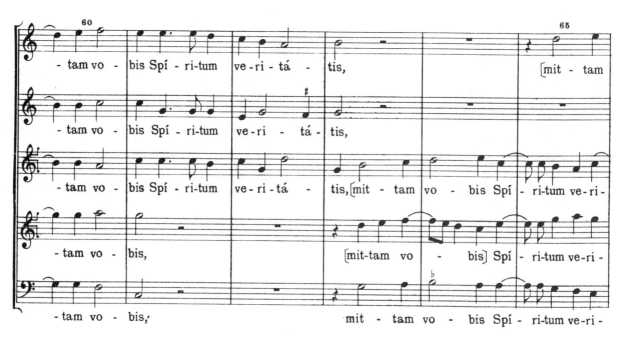

SECUNDA PARS.

da - bit vo - bis_____                          Spí - ri-tum ve-ri - tá - tis,

da - bit vo - bis]                                  Spí - ri-tum ve-ri - tá-tis,

- -bit vo - bis Spí - ri-tum ve-ri - tá - tis,_____

da - bit vo - bis Spí - ri-tum ve-ri - tá - tis,

Spí - ri-tum ve-ri - tá - tis,[Spí - ri-tum ve-ri - tá - tis,]

et gau-dé - bit,      [et gau-dé - bit]   cor   ve - 

et gau-dé - bit,      et gau-dé - bit   cor   ve - 

et   gau-dé - bit, [et gau-dé - bit,]

et gau-dé - bit, [et gau-dé - bit,]      [et gau-dé - bit,]

et gau-dé - bit,           [et gau-dé - bit,]

strum,                              et   gau-dé - bit cor      ve - 

strum,                      [et   gau-dé - bit   cor   ve - 

et gau-dé - bit cor      ve - strum,et gau-dé - bit cor ve-

[et gau-dé - bit] cor   ve - strum,            [cor ve - 

[et gau-dé - bit] cor ve - strum.

# Missa Ascendo ad Patrem

*MASS FOR 5 VOICES*

## Kyrie

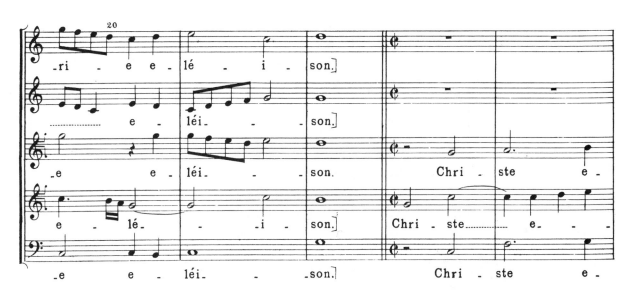

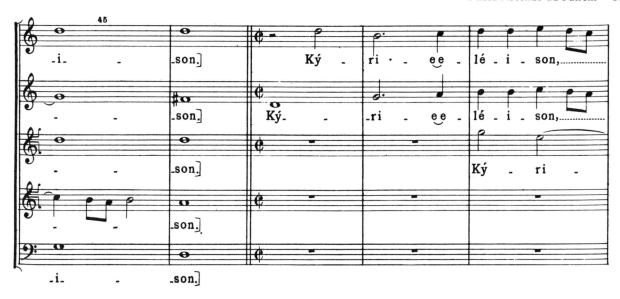

# Gloria

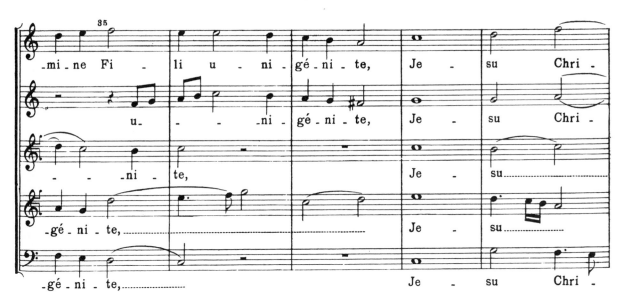

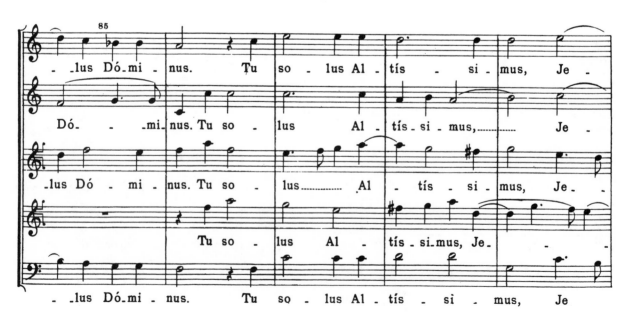

Pa_tris._____ A_men.

_tris.    A_____men,_____ a_____men.

_a De_i    Pa_tris. A_____men, a_____men.

_a De_i    Pa_tris.    A_____men.

Pa_    tris.    A_____men,    a_____men.

# Credo

**CANTUS**

Pa_____trem    o_mni_po_tén_____tem,

**ALTUS**

Pa_____trem_____o_mni_po_tén_____tem,

**TENOR I**

Pa_____trem    o_mni_po_tén_____tem, fa_ctó_rem

**TENOR II**
(Quintus)

Pa_____trem_____o_mni_po_tén_____tem, fa_ctó_rem

**BASSUS**

fa_ctó_rem coe_li    et    ter_rae,    vi_____si_bí_li_

fa_ctó_rem coe_li    et    ter_____rae,    vi_si_bí_li_

coe_____li et_____ter_rae,

coe_____li et    ter_rae,_____vi_____si_bí_li

coe_____li    et    ter_rae,_____vi_____si_bí_li

fa_ctó_rem coe_li    et    ter_____rae,    vi_si_bí_li

Et in — car_ná_tus est de Spí_ri_tu San_cto, ex— Ma_rí_

Et in — car_ná_tus est de Spí_ri_tu— San_cto, ex Ma_rí_

Et in — car_ná_tus est de Spí_ri_tu San_cto,

ex Ma_rí_

Et in — car_ná_tus est de Spí_ri_tu San_cto,

_a Vír_gi_ne: et ho_mo fa_ctus est.

_a Vír_gi_ne: et ho_mo fa_ctus est.

et ho_mo fa_ _ctus est.

_a Vír_gi_ne: et ho_mo fa_ctus est.

et ho_mo fa_ctus est.

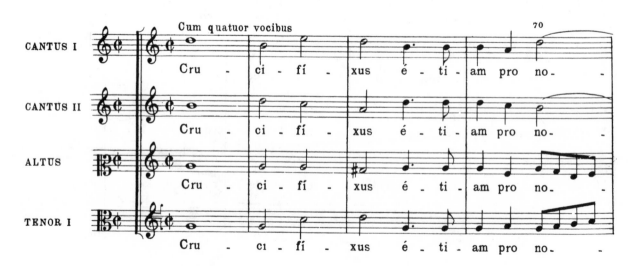

**CANTUS I**  Cum quatuor vocibus
Cru — ci — fí — xus é — ti_am pro no_ _

**CANTUS II**  Cru — ci — fí — xus é — ti_am pro no_ _

**ALTUS**  Cru — ci — fí — xus é — ti_am pro no_ _

**TENOR I**  Cru — ci — fí — xus é — ti_am pro no_ _

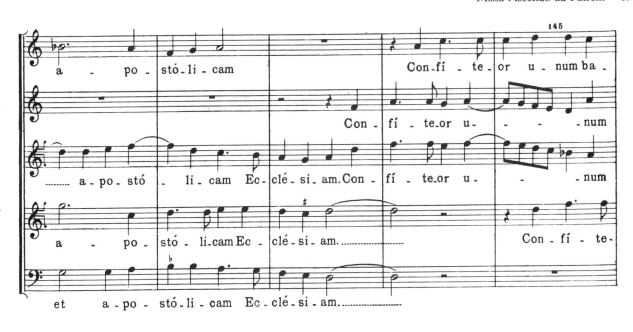

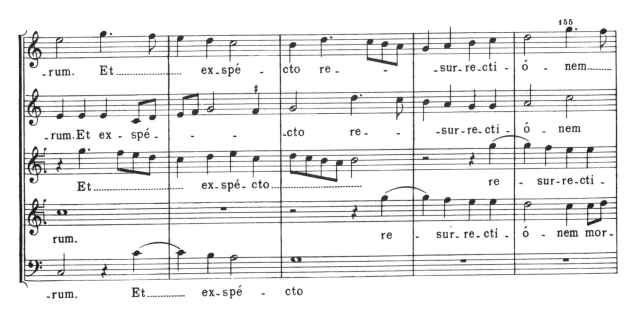

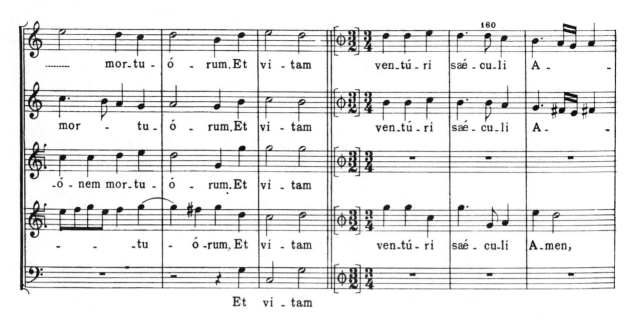

# Sanctus

# Benedictus

## Agnus Dei I

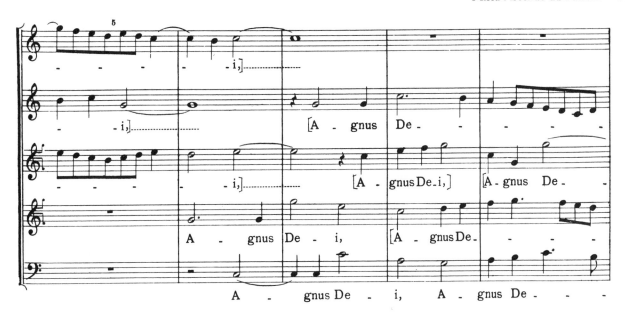

# Agnus Dei II

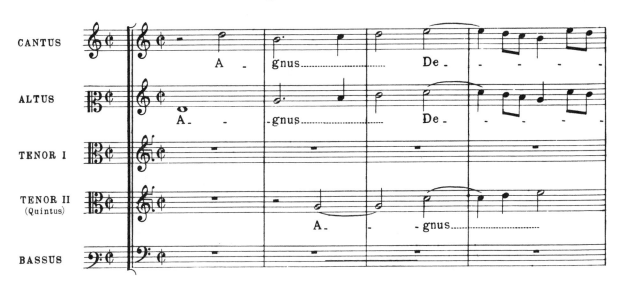

# Missa L'Homme Armé

## MASS FOR 5 VOICES

### Kyrie.

## Gloria.

## Credo.

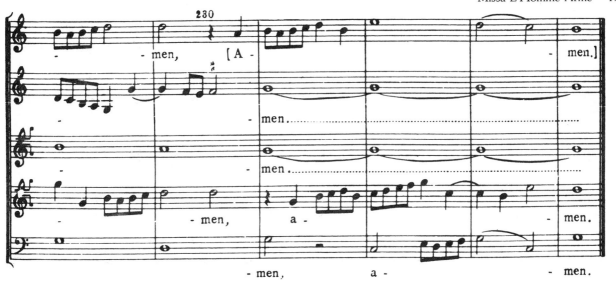

## Sanctus

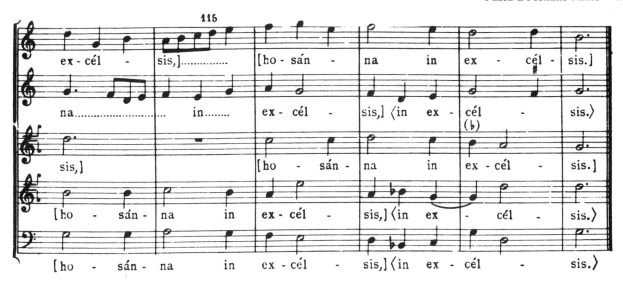

## Benedictus.

Hosánna *ut supra.*

# Agnus Dei I.

# Agnus Dei II.

# Missa Papae Marcelli

## *MASS FOR 6 VOICES*

### Kyrie

## Gloria

# Credo

## Sanctus

# Benedictus

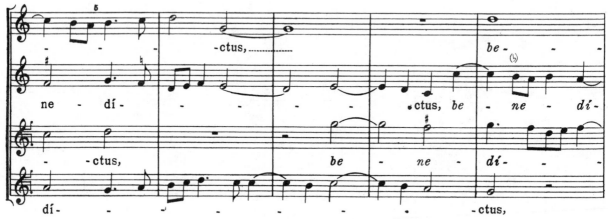

Hosánna, *ut supra.*

# Agnus Dei I.

# Agnus Dei II.
## 7 VOCUM

THE END

**ELEVEN GREAT CANTATAS, J. S. Bach.** Full vocal-instrumental score from Bach-Gesellschaft edition. *Christ lag in Todesbanden, Ich hatte viel Bekümmerniss, Jauchhzet Gott in allen Landen,* eight others. Study score. 350pp. 9 × 12. 23268-9 Pa. **$14.95**

**SEVEN GREAT SACRED CANTATAS IN FULL SCORE, Johann Sebastian Bach.** Seven favorite sacred cantatas. Printed from a clear, modern engraving and sturdily bound; new literal line-for-line translations. Reliable Bach-Gesellschaft edition. Complete German texts. 256pp. 9 × 12. 24950-6 Pa. **$12.95**

**SIX GREAT SECULAR CANTATAS IN FULL SCORE, Johann Sebastian Bach.** Bach's nearest approach to comic opera. *Hunting Cantata, Wedding Cantata, Aeolus Appeased, Phoebus and Pan, Coffee Cantata,* and *Peasant Cantata.* 286pp. 9 × 12. 23934-9 Pa. **$13.95**

**MASS IN B MINOR IN FULL SCORE, Johann Sebastian Bach.** The crowning glory of Bach's lifework in the field of sacred music and a universal statement of Christian faith, reprinted from the authoritative Bach-Gesellschaft edition. Translation of texts. 320pp. 9 × 12. 25992-7 Pa. **$12.95**

**GIULIO CESARE IN FULL SCORE, George Frideric Handel.** Great Baroque masterpiece reproduced directly from authoritative Deutsche Handelgesellschaft edition. Gorgeous melodies, inspired orchestration. Complete and unabridged. 160pp. 9⅜ × 12¼. 25056-3 Pa. **$9.95**

**MESSIAH IN FULL SCORE, George Frideric Handel.** An authoritative full-score edition of the oratorio that is the best-known, most beloved, most performed large-scale musical work in the English-speaking world. 240pp. 9 × 12. 26067-4 Pa. **$11.95**

**REQUIEM IN FULL SCORE, Wolfgang Amadeus Mozart.** Masterpiece of vocal composition, among the most recorded and performed works in the repertoire. Authoritative edition published by Breitkopf & Härtel, Wiesbaden, n.d. 203pp. 8⅜ × 11¼. 25311-2 Pa. **$7.95**

**COSI FAN TUTTE IN FULL SCORE, Wolfgang Amadeus Mozart.** Scholarly edition of one of Mozart's greatest operas. Da Ponte libretto. Commentary. Preface. Translated frontmatter. 448pp. 9⅜ × 12¼. (Available in U.S. only) 24528-4 Pa. **$17.95**

**THE MARRIAGE OF FIGARO: COMPLETE SCORE, Wolfgang A. Mozart.** Finest comic opera ever written. Full score, not to be confused with piano renderings. Peters edition. Study score. 448pp. 9⅜ × 12¼. (Available in U.S. only) 23751-6 Pa. **$17.95**

**DON GIOVANNI: COMPLETE ORCHESTRAL SCORE, Wolfgang A. Mozart.** Full score, not to be confused with piano reductions. All optional numbers, much material not elsewhere. Peters edition. Study score. 468pp. 9⅜ × 12¼. (Available in U.S. only) 23026-0 Pa. **$19.95**

**THE ABDUCTION FROM THE SERAGLIO IN FULL SCORE, Wolfgang Amadeus Mozart.** Mozart's early comic masterpiece, exactingly reproduced from the authoritative Breitkopf & Härtel edition. 320pp. 9 × 12. 26004-6 Pa. **$12.95**

**THE MAGIC FLUTE (DIE ZAUBERFLÖTE) IN FULL SCORE, Wolfgang Amadeus Mozart.** Authoritative C. F. Peters edition of Mozart's last opera featuring all the spoken dialogue. Translation of German frontmatter. Dramatis personae. List of Numbers. 226pp. 9 × 12. 24783-X Pa. **$11.95**

**THE SEASONS IN FULL SCORE, Joseph Haydn.** A masterful coda to a prolific career, this brilliant oratorio—Haydn's last major work. Unabridged republication of the work as published by C. F. Peters, Leipzig, n.d. English translation of frontmatter. 320pp. 9 × 12. 25022-9 Pa. **$14.95**

**FIDELIO IN FULL SCORE, Ludwig van Beethoven.** Beethoven's only opera, complete in one affordable volume, including all spoken German dialogue. Republication of C. F. Peters, Leipzig edition. 272pp. 9 × 12. 24740-6 Pa. **$13.95**

**THE BARBER OF SEVILLE IN FULL SCORE, Gioacchino Rossini.** One of the greatest comic operas ever written, reproduced here directly from the authoritative score published by Ricordi. 464pp. 8⅜ × 11¼. 26019-4 Pa. **$16.95**

**GERMAN REQUIEM IN FULL SCORE, Johannes Brahms.** Definitive Breitkopf & Härtel edition of Brahms's greatest vocal work, fully scored for solo voices, mixed chorus and orchestra. 208pp. 9⅜ × 12¼. 25486-0 Pa. **$10.95**

**REQUIEM IN FULL SCORE, Giuseppe Verdi.** Immensely popular with choral groups and music lovers. Republication of edition published by C. F. Peters, Leipzig, n.d. Study score. 204pp. 9⅜ × 12¼. (Available in U.S. only) 23682-X Pa. **$10.95**

**OTELLO IN FULL SCORE, Giuseppe Verdi.** The penultimate Verdi opera, his tragic masterpiece. Complete unabridged score from authoritative Ricordi edition, with frontmatter translated. 576pp. 8¼ × 11. 25040-7 Pa. **$21.95**

**FALSTAFF, Giuseppe Verdi.** Verdi's last great work, first and only comedy. Complete unabridged score from original Ricordi edition. 480pp. 8⅜ × 11¼. 24017-7 Pa. **$17.95**

**AÏDA IN FULL SCORE, Giuseppe Verdi.** Verdi's most popular opera in an authoritative edition from G. Ricordi of Milan. 448pp. 9 × 12. 26172-7 Pa. **$17.95**

**LA BOHÈME IN FULL SCORE, Giacomo Puccini.** Authoritative Italian edition of one of the world's most beloved operas. English translations of list of characters and instruments. 416pp. 8⅜ × 11¼. 25477-1 Pa. **$16.95**

**DER FREISCHÜTZ, Carl Maria von Weber.** Full orchestral score to first Romantic opera, path-breaker for later developments, Wagner. Still very popular. Study score, including full spoken text. 203pp. 9 × 12. 23449-5 Pa. **$10.95**

**CARMEN IN FULL SCORE, Georges Bizet.** Complete, authoritative score of what is perhaps the world's most popular opera, in the version most commonly performed today, with recitatives by Ernest Guiraud. 574pp. 9 × 12. 25820-3 Pa. **$19.95**

**DAS RHEINGOLD IN FULL SCORE, Richard Wagner.** Complete score, clearly reproduced from authoritative B. Schott's edition. New translation of German frontmatter. 328pp. 9 × 12. 24925-5 Pa. **$14.95**

**DIE WALKÜRE, Richard Wagner.** Complete orchestral score of the most popular of the operas in the Ring Cycle. Reprint of the edition published in Leipzig by C. F. Peters, ca. 1910. Study score. 710pp. 8⅜ × 11¼. 23566-1 Pa. **$24.95**

**SIEGFRIED IN FULL SCORE, Richard Wagner.** *Siegfried,* third opera of Wagner's famous *Ring,* is reproduced from first edition (1876). 439pp. 9⅜ × 12¼. 24456-3 Pa. **$16.95**

**GÖTTERDÄMMERUNG, Richard Wagner.** Full operatic score available in U.S. for the first time. Reprinted directly from rare 1877 first edition. 615pp. 9⅜ × 12¼. 24250-1 Pa. **$24.95**

**DIE MEISTERSINGER VON NÜRNBERG, Richard Wagner.** Landmark in history of opera in complete vocal and orchestral score. Do not confuse with piano reduction. Peters, Leipzig edition. Study score. 823pp. 8⅜ × 11. 23276-X Pa. **$28.95**

---

# *Dover Opera, Choral and Lieder Scores*

**LOHENGRIN IN FULL SCORE, Richard Wagner.** Wagner's most accessible opera. Reproduced from first engraved edition (Breitkopf & Härtel, 1887). 295pp. 9⅜ × 12¼. 24335-4 Pa. **$17.95**

**TANNHAUSER IN FULL SCORE, Richard Wagner.** Reproduces the original 1845 full orchestral and vocal score as slightly amended in 1847. Included is the ballet music for Act I written for the 1861 Paris production. 576pp. 8⅜ × 11¼. 24649-3 Pa. **$21.95**

**TRISTAN UND ISOLDE, Richard Wagner.** Full orchestral score with complete instrumentation. Study score. 655pp. 8⅛ × 11. 22915-7 Pa. **$22.95**

**PARSIFAL IN FULL SCORE, Richard Wagner.** Composer's deeply personal treatment of the legend of the Holy Grail, renowned for splendid music, glowing orchestration. C. F. Peters edition. 592pp. 8⅛ × 11. 25175-6 Pa. **$19.95**

**THE FLYING DUTCHMAN IN FULL SCORE, Richard Wagner.** Great early masterpiece reproduced directly from limited Weingartner edition (1896), incorporating Wagner's revisions. Text, stage directions in English, German, Italian. 432pp. 9⅜ × 12¼. 25629-4 Pa. **$19.95**

**BORIS GODUNOV IN FULL SCORE (Rimsky-Korsakov Version), Modest Petrovich Moussorgsky.** Russian operatic masterwork in most recorded, performed version. Authoritative Moscow edition. 784pp. 8⅜ × 11¼. 25321-X Pa. **$29.95**

**PELLÉAS ET MÉLISANDE IN FULL SCORE, Claude Debussy.** Reprinted from the E. Fromont (1904) edition, this volume faithfully reproduces the full orchestral-vocal score of Debussy's sole and enduring opera masterpiece. 416pp. 9 × 12. (Available in U.S. only) 24825-9 Pa. **$17.95**

**SALOME IN FULL SCORE, Richard Strauss.** Atmospheric color predominates in basic 20th-century work. Definitive Fürstner score, now extremely rare. 352pp. 9⅜ × 12¼. (Available in U.S. only) 24208-0 Pa. **$15.95**

**DER ROSENKAVALIER IN FULL SCORE, Richard Strauss.** First inexpensive edition of great operatic masterpiece, reprinted complete and unabridged from rare, limited Fürstner edition (1910) approved by Strauss. 528pp. 9⅜ × 12¼. (Available in U.S. only) 25498-4 Pa. **$22.95**

**DER ROSENKAVALIER: VOCAL SCORE, Richard Strauss.** Inexpensive edition reprinted directly from original Fürstner (1911) edition of vocal score. Verbal text, vocal line and piano "reduction." 448pp. 8⅜ × 11¼. (Available in U.S. only) 25501-8 Pa. **$16.95**

**THE MERRY WIDOW: Complete Score for Piano and Voice in English, Franz Lehar.** Complete score for piano and voice, reprinted directly from the first English translation (1907) published by Chappell & Co., London. 224pp. 8⅜ × 11¼. (Available in U.S. only) 24514-4 Pa. **$10.95**

**THE AUTHENTIC GILBERT & SULLIVAN SONGBOOK, W. S. Gilbert, A. S. Sullivan.** 92 songs, uncut, original keys, in piano renderings approved by Sullivan. 399pp. 9 × 12. 23482-7 Pa. **$15.95**

**MADRIGALS: BOOK IV & V, Claudio Monteverdi.** 39 finest madrigals with new English line-for-line literal translations of the poems facing the Italian text. 256pp. 8⅛ × 11. (Available in U.S. only) 25102-0 Pa. **$12.95**

**COMPLETE SONG CYCLES, Franz Schubert.** Complete piano, vocal music of *Die Schöne Müllerin, Die Winterreise, Schwanengesang*. Also Drinker English singing translations. Breitkopf & Härtel edition. 217pp. 9⅜ × 12¼. 22649-2 Pa. **$9.95**

**SCHUBERT'S SONGS TO TEXTS BY GOETHE, Franz Schubert.** Only one-volume edition of Schubert's Goethe songs from authoritative Breitkopf & Härtel edition, plus all revised versions. New prose translation of poems. 84 songs. 256pp. 9⅜ × 12¼. 23752-4 Pa. **$12.95**

**59 FAVORITE SONGS, Franz Schubert.** "Der Wanderer," "Ave Maria," "Hark, Hark, the Lark," and 56 other masterpieces of lieder reproduced from the Breitkopf & Härtel edition. 256pp. 9⅜ × 12¼. 24849-6 Pa. **$10.95**

**SONGS FOR SOLO VOICE AND PIANO, Ludwig van Beethoven.** 71 lieder, including "Adelaide," "Wonne der Wehmuth," "Die ehre Gottes aus der Natur," and famous cycle *An die ferne Geliebta*. Breitkopf & Härtel edition. 192pp. 9 × 12. 25125-X Pa. **$10.95**

**SELECTED SONGS FOR SOLO VOICE AND PIANO, Robert Schumann.** Over 100 of Schumann's greatest lieder, set to poems by Heine, Goethe, Byron, others. Breitkopf & Härtel edition. 248pp. 9⅜ × 12¼. 24202-1 Pa. **$11.95**

**THIRTY SONGS, Franz Liszt.** Selection of extremely worthwhile though not widely-known songs. Texts in French, German, and Italian, all with English translations. Piano, high voice. 144pp. 9 × 12. 23197-6 Pa. **$9.95**

**OFFENBACH'S SONGS FROM THE GREAT OPERETTAS, Jacques Offenbach.** Piano, vocal (French text) for 38 most popular songs: *Orphée, Belle Hélène, Vie Parisienne, Duchesse de Gérolstein*, others. 21 illustrations. 195pp. 9 × 12. 23341-3 Pa. **$10.95**

**SONGS, 1880–1904, Claude Debussy.** Rich selection of 36 songs set to texts by Verlaine, Baudelaire, Pierre Louys, Charles d'Orleans, others. 175pp. 9 × 12. 24131-9 Pa. **$8.95**

**THE COMPLETE MÖRIKE SONGS, Hugo Wolf.** Splendid settings of 53 poems by Eduard Mörike. "Der Tambour," "Elfenlied," "Verborganheit," 50 more. New prose translations. 208pp. 9⅜ × 12¼. 24380-X Pa. **$11.95**

**SPANISH AND ITALIAN SONGBOOKS, Hugo Wolf.** Total of 90 songs by great 19th-century master of the genre. Reprint of authoritative C. F. Peters edition. New Translations of German texts. 256pp. 9⅜ × 12¼. 26156-5 Pa. **$12.95**

**SIXTY SONGS, Gabriel Fauré.** "Clair de lune," "Apres un reve," "Chanson du pecheur," "Automne," and other great songs set for medium voice. Reprinted from French editions. 288pp. 8⅜ × 11. (Not available in France or Germany) 26534-X Pa. **$13.95**

**FRENCH ART SONGS OF THE NINETEENTH-CENTURY, Philip Hale (ed.).** 39 songs from romantic period by 18 composers: Berioz, Chausson, Debussy (six songs), Gounod, Massenet, Thomas, etc. For high voice, French text, English singing translation. 182pp. 9 × 12. (Not available in France or Germany) 23680-3 Pa. **$9.95**

**COMPLETE SONGS FOR SOLO VOICE AND PIANO (two volumes), Johannes Brahms.** A total of 113 songs in complete score by greatest lieder writer since Schubert. Volume I contains 15-song cycle Die Schone Magelone; Volume II famous "Lullaby." Total of 448pp. 9⅜ × 12¼. Volume I 23820-2 Pa. **$11.95**
Volume II 23821-0 Pa. **$11.95**

**COMPLETE SONGS FOR SOLO VOICE AND PIANO: Series III, Johannes Brahms.** 64 songs, published between 1877–86, including such favorites as "Geheimnis," "Alte Liebe," and "Vergebliches Standchen." 224pp. 9 × 12. 23822-9 Pa. **$11.95**

**COMPLETE SONGS FOR SOLO VOICE AND PIANO: Series IV, Johannes Brahms.** 120 songs that complete the Brahms song oeuvre and sensitive arrangements of 91 folk and traditional songs. 240pp. 9 × 12. 23823-7 Pa. **$11.95**

*Available from your music dealer or write for **free** Music Catalog to Dover Publications, Inc., Dept. MUBI, 31 East 2nd Street, Mineola, N.Y. 11501.*

# *Dover Chamber Music Scores*

**COMPLETE SUITES FOR UNACCOMPANIED CELLO AND SONATAS FOR VIOLA DA GAMBA, Johann Sebastian Bach.** Bach-Gesellschaft edition of the six cello suites (BWV 1007–1012) and three sonatas (BWV 1027–1029), commonly played today on the cello. 112pp. 9⅜ × 12¼. 25641-3 Pa. **$8.95**

**WORKS FOR VIOLIN, Johann Sebastian Bach.** Complete Sonatas and Partitas for Unaccompanied Violin; Six Sonatas for Violin and Clavier. Bach-Gesellschaft edition. 158pp. 9⅜ × 12¼. 23683-8 Pa. **$8.95**

**COMPLETE STRING QUARTETS, Wolfgang A. Mozart.** Breitkopf & Härtel edition. All 23 string quartets plus alternate slow movement to K.156. Study score. 277pp. 9⅜ × 12¼. 22372-8 Pa. **$12.95**

**COMPLETE STRING QUINTETS, Wolfgang Amadeus Mozart.** All the standard-instrumentation string quintets, plus String Quintet in C Minor, K.406; Quintet with Horn or Second Cello, K.407; and Clarinet Quintet, K.581. Breitkopf & Härtel edition. Study score. 181pp. 9⅜ × 12¼. 23603-X Pa. **$8.95**

**STRING QUARTETS, OPP. 20 and 33, COMPLETE, Joseph Haydn.** Complete reproductions of the 12 masterful quartets (six each) of Opp. 20 and 33—in the reliable Eulenburg edition. 272pp. 8⅜ × 11¼. 24852-6 Pa. **$12.95**

**STRING QUARTETS, OPP. 42, 50 and 54, Joseph Haydn.** Complete reproductions of Op. 42 in D minor; Op. 50, Nos. 1–6 ("Prussian Quartets") and Op. 54, Nos. 1–3. Reliable Eulenburg edition. 224pp. 8⅜ × 11¼. 24262-5 Pa. **$11.95**

**TWELVE STRING QUARTETS, Joseph Haydn.** 12 often-performed works: Op. 55, Nos. 1–3 (including *Razor*); Op. 64, Nos. 1–6; Op. 71, Nos. 1–3. Definitive Eulenburg edition. 288pp. 8⅜ × 11¼. 23933-0 Pa. **$11.95**

**ELEVEN LATE STRING QUARTETS, Joseph Haydn.** Complete reproductions of Op. 74, Nos. 1–3; Op. 76, Nos. 1–6; and Op. 77, Nos. 1 and 2. Definitive Eulenburg edition. Full-size study score. 320pp. 8⅜ × 11¼. 23753-2 Pa. **$12.95**

**COMPLETE STRING QUARTETS, Ludwig van Beethoven.** Breitkopf & Härtel edition. Six quartets of Opus 18; three quartets of Opus 59; Opera 74, 95, 127, 130, 131, 132, 135 and Grosse Fuge. Study score. 434pp. 9⅜ × 12¼. 22361-2 Pa. **$15.95**

**SIX GREAT PIANO TRIOS IN FULL SCORE, Ludwig van Beethoven.** Definitive Breitkopf & Härtel edition of Beethoven's Piano Trios Nos. 1–6 including the "Ghost" and the "Archduke". 224pp. 9⅜ × 12¼. 25398-8 Pa. **$10.95**

**COMPLETE VIOLIN SONATAS, Ludwig van Beethoven.** All ten sonatas including the "Kreutzer" and "Spring" sonatas in the definitive Breitkopf & Härtel edition. 256pp. 9 × 12. 26277-4 Pa. **$12.95**

**COMPLETE SONATAS AND VARIATIONS FOR CELLO AND PIANO, Ludwig van Beethoven.** All five sonatas and three sets of variations. Reprinted from Breitkopf & Härtel edition. 176pp. 9⅜ × 12¼. 26441-6 Pa. **$10.95**

**COMPLETE CHAMBER MUSIC FOR STRINGS, Franz Schubert.** Reproduced from famous Breitkopf & Härtel edition: Quintet in C Major (1828), 15 quartets and two trios for violin(s), viola, and violincello. Study score. 348pp. 9 × 12. 21463-X Pa. **$14.95**

**COMPLETE CHAMBER MUSIC FOR PIANOFORTE AND STRINGS, Franz Schubert.** Breitkopf & Härtel edition. *Trout*, Quartet in F Major, and trios for piano, violin, cello. Study score. 192pp. 9 × 12. 21527-X Pa. **$9.95**

**CHAMBER WORKS FOR PIANO AND STRINGS, Felix Mendelssohn.** Eleven of the composer's best known works in the genre—duos, trios, quartets and a sextet—reprinted from authoritative Breitkopf & Härtel edition. 384pp. 9⅜ × 12¼. 26117-4 Pa. **$15.95**

**COMPLETE CHAMBER MUSIC FOR STRINGS, Felix Mendelssohn.** All of Mendelssohn's chamber music: Octet, Two Quintets, Six Quartets, and Four Pieces for String Quartet. (Nothing with piano is included). Complete works edition (1874–7). Study score. 283pp. 9⅜ × 12¼. 23679-X Pa. **$12.95**

**CHAMBER MUSIC OF ROBERT SCHUMANN, edited by Clara Schumann.** Superb collection of three trios, four quartets, and piano quintet. Breitkopf & Härtel edition. 288pp. 9⅜ × 12¼. 24101-7 Pa. **$12.95**

**COMPLETE SONATAS FOR SOLO INSTRUMENT AND PIANO, Johannes Brahms.** All seven sonatas—three for violin, two for cello and two for clarinet (or viola)—reprinted from the authoritative Breitkopf & Härtel edition. 208pp. 9 × 12. 26091-7 Pa. **$11.95**

**COMPLETE CHAMBER MUSIC FOR STRINGS AND CLARINET QUINTET, Johannes Brahms.** Vienna Gesellschaft der Musikfreunde edition of all quartets, quintets, and sextet without piano. Study edition. 262pp. 8⅜ × 11¼. 21914-3 Pa. **$11.95**

**QUINTET AND QUARTETS FOR PIANO AND STRINGS, Johannes Brahms.** Full scores of *Quintet in F Minor*, Op. 34; *Quartet in G Minor*, Op. 25; *Quartet in A Major*, Op. 26; *Quartet in C Minor*, Op. 60. Breitkopf & Härtel edition. 298pp. 9 × 12. 24900-X Pa. **$13.95**

**COMPLETE PIANO TRIOS, Johannes Brahms.** All five piano trios in the definitive Breitkopf & Härtel edition. 288pp. 9 × 12. 25769-X Pa. **$13.95**

**CHAMBER WORKS FOR PIANO AND STRINGS, Antonín Dvorák.** Society editions of the F Minor and Dumky piano trios, D Major and E-flat Major piano quartets and A Major piano quintet. 352pp. 8⅜ × 11¼. (Available in U.S. only) 25663-4 Pa. **$15.95**

**FIVE LATE STRING QUARTETS, Antonín Dvorák.** Treasury of Czech master's finest chamber works: Nos. 10, 11, 12, 13, 14. Reliable Simrock editions. 282pp. 8⅛ × 11. 25135-7 Pa. **$11.95**

**STRING QUARTETS BY DEBUSSY AND RAVEL/Claude Debussy: Quartet in G Minor, Op. 10/Maurice Ravel: Quartet in F Major, Claude Debussy and Maurice Ravel.** Authoritative one-volume edition of two influential masterpieces noted for individuality, delicate and subtle beauties. 112pp. 8⅛ × 11. (Not available in France or Germany) 25231-0 Pa. **$7.95**

**GREAT CHAMBER WORKS, César Franck.** Four Great works: Violin Sonata in A Major, Piano Trio in F-sharp Minor, String Quartet in D Major and Piano Quintet in F Minor. From J. Hamelle, Paris and C. F. Peters, Leipzig editions. 248pp. 9⅜ × 12¼. **26546-3 Pa. $13.95**

*Available from your music dealer or write for **free** Music Catalog to Dover Publications, Inc., Dept. MUBI, 31 East 2nd Street, Mineola, N.Y. 11501.*